MR. MEN™ LITTLE MISS™ © THOIP (a SANRIO company)

Mr Greedy Eats Clean to Get Lean © 2017 THOIP (a SANRIO company)
Printed and published under licence from Price Stern Sloan, Inc., Los Angeles.
Published in Great Britain by Egmont UK Limited
The Yellow Building, 1 Nicholas Road, London W11 4AN

ISBN 978 1 4052 8870 5
68154/1
Printed in Italy

MR. GREEDY
EATS CLEAN TO
GET LEAN

Original concept and illustrations by
Roger Hargreaves

Written by
Sarah Daykin, Lizzie Daykin and Liz Bankes

EGMONT

Mr Greedy liked to eat!

In fact, Mr Greedy loved to eat. But the older he got the fatter he got.

And the more he drank, the fatter he got.

And the longer he was married, the fatter he got.

Until his middle-aged spread had spread so much that he stopped wearing clothes altogether!

Mr Greedy lived in Fatland, where everyone loved their food. They liked nothing more than devouring a cheeky bhuna, downing a cheeky wine, and demolishing a cheeky cheeseboard. Followed by a cheeky bottle of Gaviscon the next day.

But things were changing . . .

It all began when Mr Small started juicing.

Then Mr Muddle read somewhere that it only took 15 minutes to get lean.

So he spent ten minutes exercising.

And five minutes posting pictures of himself in the gym.

Then he got himself some personal trainers.

#mrmenwholift #iaminthegym #pleaselikeme #lookatmyshoes

And Mr Tickle was on the 5:2 diet.

Unfortunately he'd got it wrong and had fasted for 52 days straight.

He lost so much weight in such a short amount of time that his arms were now mostly loose skin.

Mr Greedy thought it was all rather silly. One day he was in the park, thinking how silly it all was, when he saw his friend Mr Worry walking very quickly.

'9993, 9994, 9995 . . .' counted Mr Worry.

'Morning!' said Mr Greedy.

'Don't interrupt me!' said Mr Worry. 'I'm counting my 10,000 steps. I read in the Daily Fearmongerer that if you don't count them it's really bad for you.'

'Oh right!' chuckled Mr Greedy. 'Shall we have breakfast when you're done?'

'Breakfast takes ten years off your life!' panicked Mr Worry. 'I must go!'

And off he went again. '1, 2, 3 . . .'

At least Mr Greedy had Mrs Greedy.

'Here's my jellybean!' she said as he got home. 'I got you a treat.'

Mr Greedy peeked in the box.

And what do you think he found? Black forest gâteaux? Jam donuts? Chocolate éclairs?

Courgette cake!!!!

Why would she get him something so . . . green?

Mr Greedy had strong views on vegetables masquerading as cakes.

Had she been brainwashed too? Surely not!

Come to think of it she had been hiding the biscuit tin.
And she had been leaving gym leaflets around the house.
And she did keep talking about her colleague Mr Perfect,
who cycled everywhere and still had all his own hair.

Was she trying to tell him something?

He was sure it was fine and she wasn't having an affair
. . . but just to be on the safe side he decided to become
an irresistible muscle-bound god.

Luckily, just at that moment, he saw an advert for
Mr Strong's Bootcamp.

ARE YOU GETTING *FAT, OLD* AND *BALD?*
DOES YOUR TUMMY HAVE SO MANY ROLLS
YOU COULD OPEN A BAKERY?

Sign up to Mr Strong's bootcamp and get square in no time!*

DON'T JUST TAKE OUR WORD FOR IT:
'I was bullied at school – now I can tie a knot in an iron bar.'
Mr Strong, aged 37.

*May take a lot of time

So Mr Greedy went to bootcamp, which for absolutely no reason started at 6am on a Saturday.

'BOOTCAMP STARTS WITH PROTEIN!' shouted Mr Strong.

73 raw eggs later, all Mr Greedy had done was a load of burpees and been sick on the floor.

'KEEP GOING!' bellowed Mr Strong. 'DON'T YOU WANT TO BE ABLE TO TIE A KNOT IN AN IRON BAR?'

'Not really. What's the point?' said Mr Greedy.

'Because . . .' Mr Strong fell silent. For the first time in his life he questioned his entire existence.

Then he quickly overcompensated by pushing over a tree and yelling, 'TESTOSTERONE!'

The only pounds Mr Greedy had lost were the 350 he'd spent on the bootcamp joining fee.

'At least I tried,' he shrugged.

Heading home he bumped into Mr Perfect, who was busy doing squats. Mr Perfect had perfect hair, a perfect smile and perfectly fitting cycling shorts that revealed a lot about him.

He stood up and appeared to be holding something he'd deposited while squatting.

'Energy ball?' he said.

'No thanks.'

Mr Greedy was greedy, but even he had limits.

After begrudgingly sponsoring Mr Perfect fifty quid for Tough-Mr-Mudder, Mr Greedy decided to give fitness one more go. He went to see Little Miss Somersault.

She was busy balancing an interior design business, raising six gifted children, teaching yoga and building her lifestyle brand, Clean Living Guru™.

'I treat my body like a temple which means I clean everything!' said Little Miss Somersault as she cleaned Mr Greedy from top to his bottom. 'You simply buy food that is whole, unprocessed and direct from the health food shop.'

'Okay,' said Mr Greedy.

'And then you put it in the dishwasher,' said Little Miss Somersault. 'Just to make sure it's extra clean.'

She was just on a call from one of her many celebrity clients, when all of a sudden, she cocked her leg in the air and bent over backwards.

'Are you alright?' asked Mr Greedy.

'I'm fine!' she replied. 'I'm just doing the upward-facing farting dog.'

Nothing was working.

He even tried calling in on Mr Clumsy, who had recently gone gluten-free . . .

. . . but it wasn't a good time.

'What's the matter?' said Mrs Greedy at dinner that evening. 'You haven't touched your fava beans.'

Mr Greedy explained how he had been trying to lose weight so that she'd fancy him again.

'Fancy you? Of course I fancy you!' she said.

And then Mrs Greedy explained that *she'd* been trying to lose weight so *he'd* fancy *her* again.

'Fancy you? Of course I fancy you!' he said.

'So we both fancy each other?' they both said together.

And with that, Mrs Greedy chucked the fava beans in the bin and hugged Mr Greedy's roly-poly tummy.

Then Mrs Greedy had a splendid idea to make them both feel better.

She invited Mr and Mrs Giant from next door round for dinner!

And do you know, from that day to this, Mr Greedy never felt big again.

So, if you're as greedy as Mr Greedy, you know what to do, don't you?'

Find some bigger friends!

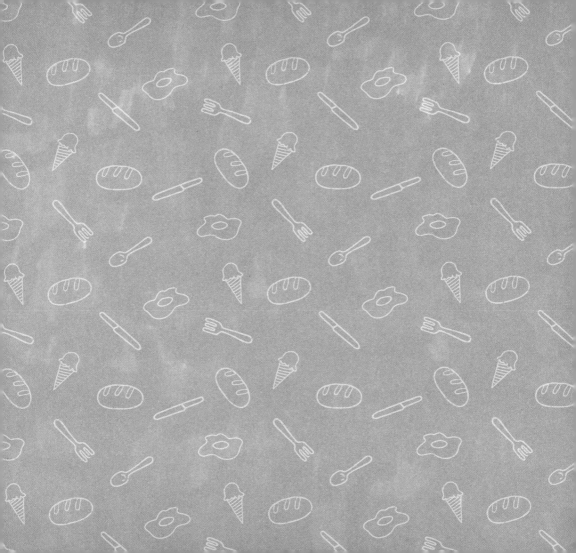